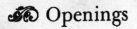 Openings

Also by Wendell Berry

OPENINGS

Poems by Wendell Berry

A Harvest/HBJ Book

Harcourt Brace Jovanovich

New York and London

Some of the poems in this volume previously appeared
in *Appalachian Review*, *Arts and Sciences* (New York University),
Beloit Poetry Journal, *Broadside*, the Catalogue of an Exhibition
of the Paintings of Stuart Egnal, Department of Fine Arts,
University of Pennsylvania, *Chelsea*, *Commonweal*, *Epoch*,
Hiram Poetry Review, *The Hudson Review*, *Kayak*, *Monk's Pond*,
The Nation, the New York *Times*, *Poetry Northwest*,
Religious Humanism, *Southern Poetry Review*, and *The Virginia
Quarterly Review*. "The Porch Over the River," "Grace,"
"To Think of the Life of a Man," "Marriage,"
"The Dead Calf," "The Burial of the Old,"
"Do Not Be Ashamed," and "Window Poems" 2, 15, 16,
18, 19, 20, 21 and 26 appeared originally in *Poetry*.

Library of Congress Cataloging in Publication Data

Berry, Wendell, 1934–
Openings : poems.

(A Harvest/HBJ book)
I.   Title.
[PS3552.E75O6   1980]   811'.54   80-15552
ISBN 0-15-670012-3

Printed in the United States of America

First Harvest/HBJ edition 1980

A B C D E F G H I J

For Tanya

Contents

Openings

✌ The Thought of Something Else

1.

A spring wind blowing
the smell of the ground
through the intersections of traffic,
the mind turns, seeks a new
nativity—another place,
simpler, less weighted
by what has already been.

Another place!
it's enough to grieve me—
that old dream of going,
of becoming a better man
just by getting up and going
to a better place.

2.

The mystery. The old
unaccountable unfolding.
The iron trees in the park
suddenly remember forests.
It becomes possible to think of going

3.

—a place where thought
can take its shape
as quietly in the mind
as water in a pitcher,

or a man can be
safely without thought
—see the day begin
and lean back,
a simple wakefulness filling
perfectly
the spaces among the leaves.

✒ My Great-Grandfather's Slaves

Deep in the back ways of my mind I see them
    going in the long days
    over the same fields that I have gone
    long days over.

I see the sun passing and burning high
    over that land from their day
    until mine, their shadows
    having risen and consumed them.

I see them obeying and watching
    the bearded tall man whose voice
    and blood are mine, whose countenance
    in stone at his grave my own resembles,
    whose blindness is my brand.

I see them kneel and pray to the white God
    who buys their souls with Heaven.

I see them approach, quiet
    in the merchandise of their flesh,
    to put down their burdens
    of firewood and hemp and tobacco
    into the minds of my kinsmen.

I see them moving in the rooms of my history,
    the day of my birth entering
    the horizon emptied of their days,
    their purchased lives taken back
    into the dust of birthright.

I see them borne, shadow within shadow,
    shroud within shroud, through all nights
    from their lives to mine, long beyond
    reparation or given liberty
    or any straightness.

I see them go in the bonds of my blood
        through all the time of their bodies.

I have seen that freedom cannot be taken
        from one man and given to another,
        and cannot be taken and kept.

I know that freedom can only be given,
        and is the gift to the giver
        from the one who receives.

I am owned by the blood of all of them
        who ever were owned by my blood.
        We cannot be free of each other.

The Change

1.

I'll never know what causes it
—the sudden going down
into pointless sorrow, great
beyond all causes I can think of,

the almost aimless attempt
to recover out of huge darkness
the too small thought of myself.

Something turns over
in the heart, like the black
side of a mirror turned
to the light. I'm exhausted
by the thought of all
the possibilities that are lost.

2.

Now after the evening storm
the wind blows fresh off the hills,
the ripples speed against
the current, the air clears,
a kingfisher turns
the rusty hinges of his song.
The rain has left delicate lichens
clearly visible, green
on the wet trunks of the sycamores.

❧ October 10

Now constantly there is the sound,
quieter than rain,
of the leaves falling.

Under their loosening bright
gold, the sycamore limbs
bleach whiter.

Now the only flowers
are beeweed and aster, spray
of their white and lavender
over the brown leaves.

The calling of a crow sounds
loud—a landmark—now
that the life of summer falls
silent, and the nights grow.

❧ The Quiet

The fisherman rows up the river
at midmorning, anchors
outside the creek mouth.
For hours he sits there
in his boat, lines in the water,
motionless and silent
in the cool wind as a heron.

The leaves have fallen.
The rain has turned them
pliant as water.
Walking on them makes no noise.
The country has taken on
the quiet of the fisherman
fishing alone.

✣ The Snake

At the end of October
I found on the floor of the woods
a small snake whose back
was patterned with the dark
of the dead leaves he lay on.
His body was thickened with a mouse
or small bird. He was cold,
so stuporous with his full belly
and the fall air that he hardly
troubled to flicker his tongue.
I held him a long time, thinking
of the perfection of the dark
marking on his back, the death
that swelled him, his living cold.
Now the cold of him stays
in my hand, and I think of him
lying below the frost,
big with a death to nourish him
during a long sleep.

✥ White-Throated Sparrow
for *Denise and Mitchell Goodman*

1.

To draw together the differences
of minds and households as far
separate as Kentucky and Maine, we went
late in May to an old farmhouse
by rock-road and brook, surrounded
by the woods, the beginning coming back
—an old farm of the North
where summer is a smaller presence
than with us, troubled by memory
and expectancy of the huge white winter.
White-throated sparrow
was the bird of that time,
who spoke out of hiding
in clear notes like the sunlight
of spring, from which there's no subtracting
—like the clear grain of new boards
used then to build, at the top of a high
clearing, a place to work.

2.

Now gravely in Kentucky the ground
draws the leaves to it. The North
approaches it. One imagines the snow
already piling up on the hillsides of Maine,
blueberry and popple silent in the drifts.
The ties hold. Across half a continent
and half a year the memory of laughter,
intelligence suddenly breaking clear,
survives. And now the white-throated sparrow
is seen in our thickets, and we hear
a far echo of his summer song in the North.
He goes quick in the undergrowth, a spot
of sun-yellow beside his eye, scavenging seed.

❧ The Fearfulness of Hands
That Have Learned Killing

The fearfulness of hands that have learned killing
I inherit from my own life. With my hands from boyhood
I formed the small perfect movements of death,
killing for pleasure or wantonness, casually.
Manhood taught me the formal deadliness
of hunter and farmer, the shedding
of predestined blood that lives for death.
Only marrying and fathering lives
has taught me the depth of ruin,
and made me feel quick in my hands the subtlety
and warmth of what they have destroyed.
And still I have killed for pity, and felt open
in my mind the beautiful silence, the sudden
ridding of a hurt thing's pain. I
am dumbfounded at the works I have accomplished
at the bounds of mystery, seeing it flow out
red and mute, matting the hair of my hands.
The skill that is prepared in me is careful
and terrible. There is no life I can think of
without sensing in my hands the answering power.
I shall not go free of the art of death.

❦ The Cold

How exactly good it is
to know myself
in the solitude of winter,

my body containing its own
warmth, divided from all
by the cold; and to go

separate and sure
among the trees cleanly
divided, thinking of you

perfect too in your solitude,
your life withdrawn into
your own keeping

—to be clear, poised
in perfect self-suspension
toward you, as though frozen.

And having known fully the
goodness of that, it will be
good also to melt.

To My Children,
Fearing for Them

Terrors are to come. The earth
is poisoned with narrow lives.
I think of you. What you will

live through, or perish by, eats
at my heart. What have I done? I
need better answers than there are

to the pain of coming to see
what was done in blindness,
loving what I cannot save. Nor,

your eyes turning toward me,
can I wish your lives unmade
though the pain of them is on me.

&ze; The Winter Rain

The leveling of the water, its increase,
the gathering of many into much:

in the cold dusk I stop
midway of the creek, listening
as it passes downward
loud over the rocks, under
the sound of the rain striking,
nowhere any sound
but the water, the dead
weedstems soaked with it, the
ground soaked, the earth overflowing.

And having waded all the way
across, I look back and see there
on the water the still sky.

March Snow

The morning lights
whiteness that has touched the world
perfectly as air.
In the whitened country
under the still fall of the snow
only the river, like a brown earth,
taking all falling darkly
into itself, moves.

April Woods: Morning

Birth of color
out of night and the ground.

Luminous the gatherings
of bloodroot

newly risen, green leaf
white flower

in the sun, the dark
grown absent.

The Finches

The ears stung with cold
sun and frost of dawn
in early April, comes

the song of winter finches,
their crimson bright, then
dark as they move into

and then against the light.
May the year warm them
soon. May they soon go

north with their singing
and the season follow.
May the bare sticks soon

live, and our minds go free
of the ground
into the shining of trees.

❧ The Porch Over the River

In the dusk of the river, the wind
gone, the leaves grow still—
the beautiful poise of lightness,
the heavy world pushing toward it.

Beyond, on the face of the water,
lies the reflection of another tree,
inverted, pulsing with the short strokes
of waves the wind has stopped driving.

In a time when men no longer
can imagine the lives of their sons
this is still the world—
the world of my time, the grind

of engines marking the country
like an audible map, the high dark
marked by the flight of men,
lights stranger than stars.

The phoebes cross and re-cross
the openings, alert
for what may still be earned
from the light. The whippoorwills

begin, and the frogs. And the dark
falls, again, as it must.
The look of the world withdraws
into the vein of memory.

The mirrored tree, darkening, stirs
with the water's inward life. What has
made it so?—a quietness in it
no question can be asked in.

The last light gathers
on the face of the river.
Now comes the sound of wings
it has grown too dark to see.

❧ The Migrants

They depart from what they have failed
to know—old clearings overgrown
with thicket, farmlands mute
under the breath of grazing machines.

Broken from the land, they inherit
a time without history, a future
their fathers did not dream of
and they do not imagine.

Where their fathers took the hill land
the forest returns. Rains usurp the hearths.
The fear of loss dies out
as the sills drift and sink.

❧ Before Dark

From the porch at dusk I watched
a kingfisher wild in flight
he could only have made for joy.

He came down the river, splashing
against the water's dimming face
like a skipped rock, passing

on down out of sight. And still
I could hear the splashes
farther and farther away

as it grew darker. He came back
the same way, dusky as his shadow,
sudden beyond the willows.

The splashes went on out of hearing.
It was dark then. Somewhere
the night had accommodated him

—at the place he was headed for
or where, led by his delight,
he came.

❧ The Return

for Harry Caudill

1.

To re-enter
the place of beginning, the place
whose possibilities I am one of,

to return
and resume such a continuance
as there could be no other place,

to come back
to what could not be escaped—
that is to say there never was a departure.

That is to re-enter
the dust of my first flesh, and to turn
painfully against what is my own.

That is to despise wholly
what it would be half pleasing
to become.

2.

Kentucky, I know the greed and pride
that wear your fields to stone, owners who make
their graves richer than their land.

The worst that you have come to
is my worst. And I know a troubling
threatened loveliness that is in you.

And there are lives of a few men I knew,
and know still, that have taught me
that here also the best has been, and may be.

3.

I dream an inescapable dream
in which I take away from the country
the bridges and roads, the fences, the strung wires,
ourselves, all we have built and dug and hollowed out,
our flocks and herds, our droves of machines.

I restore then the wide-branching trees.
I see growing over the land and shading it
the great trunks and crowns of the first forest.
I am aware of the rattling of their branches,
the lichened channels of their bark, the saps
of the ground flowing upward to their darkness.
Like the afterimage of a light that only by not
looking can be seen, I glimpse the country as it was.
All its beings belong wholly to it. They flourish
in dying as in being born. It is the life of its deaths.

I must end, always, by replacing
our beginning there, ourselves and our blades,
the flowing in of history, putting back what I took away,
trying always with the same pain of foreknowledge
to build all that we have built, but destroy nothing.

My hands weakening, I feel on all sides blindness
growing in the land on its peering bulbous stalks.
I see that my mind is not good enough.
I see that I am eager to own the earth and to own men.
I find in my mouth a bitter taste of money,
a gaping syllable I can neither swallow nor spit out.
I see all that we have ruined in order to have, all
that was owned for a lifetime to be destroyed forever.

Where are the sleeps that escape such dreams?

4.

Who has come in the night,
tying his yacht here at the shore,
playing his radio for fear
of deep water and the dark
and the silence of his thoughts,
strewing over the rocks his imperishable
aluminum and plastic garbage?
—more rubbish in one night
than all the Shawnees made.

Who has come and gone,
leaving scattered here the litter
that was all he meant?

My neighbor and brother,
a violent brainless man
whom I must intelligently love
though I do not, or become
him, as he is.

5.

To put on again and wear
the earth of the death
of what could have been
and is not to be,
to be drawn back
by a shadowed beauty
that is vision's source
and imperative
                is to know
what one is damned to
—an anguish of the mind
turning against itself
within itself, knowledge
turning against hope
in sleeplessness, bodies
in hateful marriage.

6.

There is in my mind a place
I cannot go to, immune
from this place, a place I
have neither left nor come to,
a forest place where a stream
stands bright and still
in flowing, the light on it
going neither up nor down.

7.

In the place that is my own place, whose earth
I am shaped in and must bear, there is an old tree growing,
a great sycamore that is a wondrous healer of itself.
Fences have been tied to it, nails driven into it,
hacks and whittles cut in it, the lightning has burned it.
There is no year it has flourished in
that has not harmed it. There is a hollow in it
that is its death, though its living brims whitely
at the lip of the darkness and flows outward.
Over all its scars has come the seamless white
of the bark. It bears the gnarls of its history
healed over. It has risen to a strange perfection
in the warp and bending of its long growth.
It has gathered all accidents into its purpose.
It has become the intention and radiance of its dark fate.
It is a fact, sublime, mystical and unassailable.
In all the country there is no other like it.
I love it as I have seldom loved anything.
I recognize in it a principle, an indwelling
the same as itself, and greater, that I would be ruled by.
I see that it stands in its place, and feeds upon it,
and is fed upon, and is native, and maker.

❧ The Meadow

In the town's graveyard the oldest plot now frees itself
of sorrow, the myrtle of the graves grown wild. The last
who knew the faces who had these names are dead,
and now the names fade, dumb on the stones, wild
as shadows in the grass, clear to the rabbit and the wren.
Ungrieved, the town's ancestry fits the earth. They become
a meadow, their alien marble grown native as maple.

🙮 Against the War in Viet Nam

Believe the automatic righteousness
of whoever holds an office. Believe
the officials who see without doubt
that peace is assured by war, freedom
by oppression. The truth preserved by lying
becomes a lie, the lie the only truth.
Believe or die. For the weak
there are no potent hymns.

In the name of ourselves we ride
at the wheels of our engines,
in the name of Plenty devouring all,
the exhaust of our progress falling
deadly on villages and fields
we do not see. We are prepared
for millions of little deaths.

Where are the quiet plenteous dwellings
we were coming to, the neighborly holdings?
We see the American freedom defended
with lies, and the lies defended
with blood, the vision of Jefferson
served by the agony of children,
women cowering in holes.

✒ Dark with Power

Dark with power, we remain
the invaders of our land, leaving
deserts where forests were,
scars where there were hills.

On the mountains, on the rivers,
on the cities, on the farmlands
we lay weighted hands, our breath
potent with the death of all things.

Pray to us, farmers and villagers
of Viet Nam. Pray to us, mothers
and children of helpless countries.
Ask for nothing.

We are carried in the belly
of what we have become
toward the shambles of our triumph,
far from the quiet houses.

Fed with dying, we gaze
on our might's monuments of fire.
The world dangles from us
while we gaze.

&ctype; In Memory: Stuart Egnal

A high wooded hill near Florence, an April
afternoon. Below, the valley farms
were still and small, stall and field
hushed in brightness. Around us the woods
woke with sound, and shadows lived
in the air and on the dry leaves. You
were drawing what we saw. Its forms
and lights reached slowly to your page.
We talked, and laughed at what we said.

Fine hours. The sort men dream
of having, and of having had. Today
while I slept I saw it all
again, and words for you came to me
as though we sat there talking still
in the quick of April. A wakening
strangeness—here in another valley
you never lived to come to—half
a dialogue, keeping on.

❧ The Want of Peace

All goes back to the earth,
and so I do not desire
pride of excess or power,
but the contentments made
by men who have had little:
the fisherman's silence
receiving the river's grace,
the gardener's musing on rows.

I lack the peace of simple things.
I am never wholly in place.
I find no peace or grace.
We sell the world to buy fire,
our way lighted by burning men,
and that has bent my mind
and made me think of darkness
and wish for the dumb life of roots.

❧ The Peace of Wild Things

When despair for the world grows in me
and I wake in the night at the least sound
in fear of what my life and my children's lives may be,
I go and lie down where the wood drake
rests in his beauty on the water, and the great heron feeds.
I come into the peace of wild things
who do not tax their lives with forethought
of grief. I come into the presence of still water.
And I feel above me the day-blind stars
waiting with their light. For a time
I rest in the grace of the world, and am free.

扥 Grace

for Gurney Norman, quoting him

The woods is shining this morning.
Red, gold and green, the leaves
lie on the ground, or fall,
or hang full of light in the air still.
Perfect in its rise and in its fall, it takes
the place it has been coming to forever.
It has not hastened here, or lagged.
See how surely it has sought itself,
its roots passing lordly through the earth.
See how without confusion it is
all that it is, and how flawless
its grace is. Running or walking, the way
is the same. Be still. Be still.
"He moves your bones, and the way is clear."

᪥ To Think of the Life of a Man

In a time that breaks
in cutting pieces all around,
when men, voiceless
against thing-ridden men,
set themselves on fire, it seems
too difficult and rare
to think of the life of a man
grown whole in the world,
at peace and in place.
But having thought of it
I am beyond the time
I might have sold my hands
or sold my voice and mind
to the arguments of power
that go blind against
what they would destroy.

Marriage
to Tanya

How hard it is for me, who live
in the excitement of women
and have the desire for them
in my mouth like salt. Yet
you have taken me and quieted me.
You have been such light to me
that other women have been
your shadows. You come near me
with the nearness of sleep.
And yet I am not quiet.
It is to be broken. It is to be
torn open. It is not to be
reached and come to rest in
ever. I turn against you,
I break from you, I turn to you.
We hurt, and are hurt,
and have each other for healing.
It is healing. It is never whole.

❧ The Dead Calf

Dead at the pasture edge,
his head is without eyes, becalmed
on the grass. There was no escaping
the heaviness that came on him,
the darkness that rose
under his belly as though he stood
in a black sucking pool.
Earth's weight grew in him,
and he lay down. As he died
a great bird took his eyes.

Where is the horror in it?
Not in him, for he came to it
as a shadow into the night.
It was nameless and familiar.
He was fitted to it. In me
is where the horror is. In my mind
he does not yield. I cannot believe
the deep peace that has come to him.
I am afraid that where the light
is torn there is a wound.
There is a darkness in the soul
that loves the eyes. There is a light
in the mind that sees only light
and will not enter the darkness.

But I would have a darkness
in my mind like the dark
the dead calf makes for a time
on the grass where he lies, and will make
in the earth as he is carried down.
May all dead things lie down in me
and be at peace, as in the ground.

❧ The Burial of the Old

The old, whose bodies encrust their lives,
die, and that is well.
They unhinder what has struggled in them.

The light, painfully loved, that narrowed
and darkened in their minds
becomes again the sky.

The young, who have looked on dying,
turn back to the world, grown strangely
alert to each other's bodies.

Do Not Be Ashamed

You will be walking some night
in the comfortable dark of your yard
and suddenly a great light will shine
round about you, and behind you
will be a wall you never saw before.
It will be clear to you suddenly
that you were about to escape,
and that you are guilty: you misread
the complex instructions, you are not
a member, you lost your card
or never had one. And you will know
that they have been there all along,
their eyes on your letters and books,
their hands in your pockets,
their ears wired to your bed.
Though you have done nothing shameful,
they will want you to be ashamed.
They will want you to kneel and weep
and say you should have been like them.
And once you say you are ashamed,
reading the page they hold out to you,
then such light as you have made
in your history will leave you.
They will no longer need to pursue you.
You will pursue them, begging forgiveness.
They will not forgive you.
There is no power against them.
It is only candor that is aloof from them,
only an inward clarity, unashamed,
that they cannot reach. Be ready.
When their light has picked you out
and their questions are asked, say to them:
"I am not ashamed." A sure horizon
will come around you. The heron will begin
his evening flight from the hilltop.

✒ Window Poems

1.
Window. Window.
The wind's eye
to see into the wind.
The eye in its hollow
looking out
through the black frame
at the waves the wind
drives up the river,
whitecaps, a wild day,
the white sky
traveled by snow squalls,
the trees thrashing,
the corn blades driven,
quivering, straight out.

2.
The foliage has dropped
below the window's grave edge,
baring the sky, the distant
hills, the branches,
the year's greenness
gone down from the high
light where it so fairly
defied falling.
The country opens to the sky,
the eye purified among hard facts:
the black grid of the window,
the wood of trees branching
outward and outward
to the nervousness of twigs,
buds asleep in the air.

3.

The window has forty
panes, forty clarities
variously wrinkled, streaked
with dried rain, smudged,
dusted. The frame
is a black grid
beyond which the world
flings up the wild
graph of its growth,
tree branch, river,
slope of land,
the river passing
downward, the clouds blowing,
usually, from the west,
the opposite way.
The window is a form
of consciousness, pattern
of formed sense
through which to look
into the wild
that is a pattern too,
but dark and flowing,
bearing along the little
shapes of the mind
as the river bears
a sash of some blinded house.
This windy day
on one of the panes
a blown seed, caught
in cobweb, beats and beats.

4.

This is the wind's eye,
Wendell's window
dedicated to purposes
dark to him, a seeing into
days to come, the winds

of the days as they approach
and go by. He has come
mornings of four years
to be thoughtful here
while day and night
cold and heat
beat upon the world.
In the low room
within the weathers,
sitting at the window,
he has shed himself
at times, and been renewed.
The spark at his wrist
flickers and dies, flickers
and dies. The life in him
grows and subsides
and grows again
like the icicle throbbing
winter after winter
at a wrinkle in the eave,
flowing over itself
as it comes and goes,
fluid as a branch.

5.
Look in
and see him looking out.
He is not always
quiet, but there have been times
when happiness has come
to him, unasked,
like the stillness on the water
that holds the evening clear
while it subsides
—and he let go
what he was not.
His ancestor is the hill
that rises in the winter wind

beyond the blind wall
at his back.
It wears a patched robe
of some history that he knows
and some that he
does not: healed fields
where the woods comes back
after a time of crops,
human history
done with, a few
ragged fences surviving
among the trees;
and on the ridges still
there are open fields
where the cattle look up
to watch him on his walks
with eyes patient as time.
The hill has known
too many days and men
grown quiet behind him.
But there are mornings
when his soul emerges
from darkness
as out of a hollow in a tree
high on the crest
and takes flight
with savage joy and harsh
outcry down the long slope
of the leaves. And nights
when he sleeps sweating
under the burden of the hill.
At the window
he sits and looks out,
musing on the river,
a little brown hen duck
paddling upstream
among the windwaves
close to the far bank.
What he has understood

lies behind him
like a road in the woods. He is
a wilderness looking out
at the wild.

6.
A warm day in December,
and the rain falling
steadily through the morning
as the man works
at his table, the window
staring into the valley
as though conscious
when he is not. The cold river
steams in the warm air.
It is rising. Already
the lowest willows
stand in the water
and the swift currents
fold round them.
The bare twigs of the elms
are beaded with bright drops
that grow slowly heavy
and fall, bigger
and slower than the rain.
A fox squirrel comes
through the trees, hurrying
someplace, but it seems
to be raining everywhere,
and he submits to wetness
and sits still, miserable
maybe, for an hour.
How sheltering and clear
the window seems, the dry fireheat
inside, and outside the gray
downpour. As the man works
the weather moves
upon his mind, its dreariness
a kind of comfort.

7.

Outside the window
is a roofed wooden tray
he fills with seeds for the birds.
They make a sort of dance
as they descend and light
and fly off at a slant
across the strictly divided
black sash. At first
they came fearfully, worried
by the man's movements
inside the room. They watched
his eyes, and flew
when he looked. Now they expect
no harm from him
and forget he's there.
They come into his vision,
unafraid. He keeps
a certain distance and quietness
in tribute to them.
That they ignore him
he takes in tribute to himself.
But they stay cautious
of each other, half afraid, unwilling
to be too close. They snatch
what they can carry and fly
into the trees. They flirt out
with tail or beak and waste
more sometimes than they eat.
And the man, knowing
the price of seed, wishes
they would take more care.
But they understand only
what is free, and he
can give only as they
will take. Thus they have
enlightened him. He buys
the seed, to make it free.

8.
The river is rising,
approaching the window
in awful nearness.
Over it the air holds
a tense premonition
of the water's dark body
living where yesterday
things breathed. As he works
through the morning
the man has trouble
in the corner of his eye,
whole trees turning
in the channel as they go by,
the currents loaded
with the trash of the woods
and the trash of towns,
bearing down, and rising.

9.
There is a sort of vertical
geography that portions his life.
Outside, the chickadees
and titmice scrounge
his sunflower seed. The cardinals
feed like fires on mats of drift
lying on the currents
of the swollen river.
The air is a bridge
and they are free. He imagines
a necessary joy
in things that must fly
to eat. He is set apart
by the black grid of the window
and, below it, the table
of the contents of his mind:
notes and remnants,

uncompleted work,
unanswered mail,
unread books
—the subjects of conscience,
his yoke-fellow,
whose whispered accounting
has stopped one ear, leaving him
half deaf to the world.
Some pads of paper,
eleven pencils,
a leaky pen,
a jar of ink
are his powers. He'll
never fly.

10.

Rising, the river
is wild. There is no end
to what one may imagine
whose lands and buildings
lie in its reach. To one
who has felt his little boat
taken this way and that
in the braided currents
it is beyond speech.
"What's the river doing?"
"Coming up."
In Port Royal, that begins
A submergence of minds.
Heads are darkened.
To the man at work
through the mornings
in the long-legged cabin
above the water, there is
an influence of the rise
that he feels in his footsoles
and in his belly
even while he thinks

of something else. The window
looks out, like a word,
upon the wordless, fact
dissolving into mystery, darkness
overtaking light.
And the water reaches a height
it can only fall from, leaving
the tree trunks wet.
It has made a roof
to its rising, and become
a domestic thing.
It lies down in its place
like a horse in his stall.
Facts emerge from it:
drift it has hung in the trees,
stranded cans and bottles,
new carving in the banks
—a place of change, changed.
It leaves a mystic plane
in the air, a membrane
of history stretched between
the silt-lines on the banks,
a depth that for months
the man will go from his window
down into, knowing
he goes within the reach
of a dark power: where
the birds are, fish
were.

11.
How fine
to have a long-legged house
with a many-glassed window
looking out on the river
—and the wren singing
on a winter morning! How fine
to sweep the floor,

opening the doors
to let the air change,
and then to sit down
in the freshened room,
day pouring in the window!
But this is only for a while.
This house was not always
here. Another stood
in its place, and weathered
and grew old. He tore it down
and used the good of it
to build this. And farther on
another stood
that is gone. Nobody
alive now knows
how it looked, though some
recall a spring house
that is gone too now. The stones
strew the pasture grass
where a roan colt grazes
and lifts his head to snort
at commotions in the wind.
All passes, and the man
at work in the house
has mostly ceased to mind.
There will be pangs
of ending, and he regrets
the terrors men bring to men.
But all passes—there is even
a kind of solace in that.
He has imagined animals
grazing at nightfall
on the place where his house stands.
Already his spirit
is with them, with a strange attentiveness,
hearing the grass
quietly tearing as they graze.

12.

The country where he lives
is haunted
by the ghost of an old forest.
In the cleared fields
where he gardens
and pastures his horses
it stood once,
and will return. There will be
a resurrection of the wild.
Already it stands in wait
at the pasture fences.
It is rising up
in the waste places of the cities.
When the fools of the Capitols
have devoured each other
in righteousness,
and the machines have eaten
the rest of us, then
there will be the second coming
of the trees. They will come
straggling over the fences
slowly, but soon enough.
The highways will sound
with the feet of the wild herds,
returning. Beaver will ascend
the streams as the trees
close over them.
The wolf and the panther
will find their old ways
through the nights. Water
and air will flow clear.
Certain calamities
will have passed,
and certain pleasures.
The wind will do without
corners. How difficult
to think of it: miles and miles
and no window.

13.

Sometimes he thinks the earth
might be better without men.
He's ashamed of that.
It worries him,
him being a man, and needing
to think well of the others
in order to think well of himself.
And there are
a few he thinks well of,
a few he loves
as well as himself almost,
and he would like to say
better. But history
is so largely unforgivable.
And now his mighty government
wants to help everybody
even if it has to kill them
to do it—like the fellow in the story
who helped his neighbor to Heaven:
"I heard the Lord calling him,
Judge, and I sent him on."
According to the government
everybody is just waiting
to be given a chance
to be like us. He can't
go along with that.
Here is a thing, flesh of his flesh,
that he hates. He would like
a little assurance
that no one will destroy the world
for some good cause.
Until he dies, he would like his life
to pertain to the earth.
But there is something in him
that will wait, even
while he protests,
for things turn out as they will.
Out his window this morning

he saw nine ducks in flight,
and a hawk dive at his mate
in delight.
The day stands apart
from the calendar. There is a will
that receives it as enough.
He is given a fragment of time
in this fragment of the world.
He likes it pretty well.

14.
The longest night is past.
It is the blessed morning of the year.
Beyond the window, snow
in patches on the river bank,
frosty sunlight on the dry corn,
and buds on the water maples
red, red in the cold.

15.
The sycamore gathers
out of the sky, white
in the glance that looks up to it
through the black crisscross
of the window. But it is not a glance
that it offers itself to.
It is no lightning stroke
caught in the eye. It stays,
an old holding in place.
And its white is not so pure
as a glance would have it,
but emerges partially,
the tree's renewal of itself,
among the mottled browns
and olives of the old bark.
Its dazzling comes into the sun
a little at a time

as though a god in it
is slowly revealing himself.
How often the man of the window
has studied its motley trunk,
the out-starting of its branches,
its smooth crotches,
its revelations of whiteness,
hoping to see beyond his glances,
the distorting geometry
of preconception and habit,
to know it beyond words.
All he has learned of it
does not add up to it.
There is a bird who nests in it
in the summer and seems to sing of it—
the quick lights among its leaves
—better than he can.
It is not by his imagining
its whiteness comes.
The earth is greater than man.
To speak of it the mind must bend.

16.

His mind gone from the window
into dark thought, suddenly
a flash of water
lights in the corner of his eye:
the kingfisher is rising,
laden, out of his plunge,
the water still subsiding
under the bare willow.
The window becomes a part
of his mind's history, the entrance
of days into it. And awake
now, watching the water flow
beyond the glass, his mind
is watched by a spectre of itself
that is a window on the past.

Life steadily accumulating
its subtractions, it has fallen
to him to remember
an old man who, dying,
dreamed of his garden,
a harvest so bountiful
he couldn't carry it home
—another who saw
in the flaws of the moon
a woman's face
like a cameo.

17.

For a night and a day
his friend stayed here
on his way across the continent.
In the afternoon they walked
down from Port Royal
to the river, following
for a while the fall of Camp Branch
through the woods,
then crossing the ridge
and entering the woods again
on the valley rim. They talked
of history—men who saw visions
of crops where the woods stood
and stand again, the crops
gone. They ate the cold apples
they carried in their pockets.
They lay on a log in the sun
to rest, looking up
through bare branches at the sky.
Once, feet tangled
in an old fence of his grandfather's time
half buried in leaves, he fell
and they laughed. They saw
a nuthatch walk in a loop
on the side of a tree

in a late patch of light
while below them the *Lexington*
shoved sand up the river,
her diesels shaking the air.
They walked along trees
across ravines. Now his friend
is back on the highway, and he sits again
at his window. Another day.
During the night snow fell.

18.

The window grows fragile
in a time of war.
The man seated beneath it
feels its glass turn deadly.
He feels the nakedness
of his face and throat.
Its shards and splinters balance
in transparence, delicately
seamed. In the violence
of men against men, it will not last.
In any mind turned away
in hate, it will go blind.
Men spare one another
by compact. When there is hate
it is joyous to kill. And he
has borne the hunger to destroy,
riding anger like a captain,
savage, exalted and blind.
There is war in his veins
like a loud song.
He has known his heart to rise
in glad holocaust against his kind,
and felt hard in thigh and arm
the thew of fury.

19.

Peace. May he waken
not too late from his wraths
to find his window still
clear in its wall, and the world
there. Within things
there is peace, and at the end
of things. It is the mind
turned away from the world
that turns against it.
The armed Presidents stand
on deadly islands in the air,
overshadowing the crops.
Peace. Let men, who cannot be brothers
to themselves, be brothers
to mulleins and daisies
that have learned to live on the earth.
Let them understand the pride
of sycamores and thrushes
that receive the light gladly, and do not
think to illuminate themselves.
Let them know that the foxes and the owls
are joyous in their lives,
and their gayety is praise to the heavens,
and they do not raven with their minds.
In the night the devourer,
and in the morning all things
find the light a comfort.
Peace. The earth turns
against all living, in the end.
And when mind has not outraged
itself against its nature,
they die and become the place
they lived in. Peace to the bones
that walk in the sun toward death,
for they will come to it soon enough.
Let the phoebes return in spring
and build their nest of moss
in the porch rafters,

and in autumn let them depart.
Let the garden be planted,
and let the frost come.
Peace to the porch and the garden.
Peace to the man in the window.

20.

In the early morning dark
he dreamed of the spring woodsflowers
standing in the ground,
dark yet under the leaves and under
the bare cold branches.
But in his dream he knew their way
was prepared, and in their time
they would rise up joyful.
And though he had dreamed earlier
of strife, his sleep became peaceful.
He said: If man, who has killed
his brothers and hated himself,
is made in the image of God,
then surely the bloodroot,
wild phlox, trillium and May apple
are more truly made
in God's image, for they have desired
to be no more than they are,
and they have spared each other.
Their future
is undiminished by their past.
Let me, he said in his dream,
become always less a soldier
and more a man,
for what is unopened in the ground
is pledged to peace.
When he woke and went out
a flock of wild ducks that had fed
on the river while he slept
flew off in fear of him.
And he walked, manly, into the new day.
He came to his window

where he sat and looked out,
the earth before him, blessed
by his dream of peace,
bad history behind him.

21.
He has known a tunnel
through the falling snow
that brought him back at dark
and nearly killed him on the way,
the road white as the sky
and the snow piling.
Mortality crept up close
in the darkness round his eyes.
He felt his death's wrenched avatars
lying like silent animals
along the ditch. He thought
of his wife, his supper and his bed,
and kept on, and made it.
Now he sits at the window
again, the country hard and bright
in this winter's coldest morning.
The river, unfrozen still,
gives off a breath of smoke
that flows upstream with the wind.
Behind him that burrow
along the wild road
grows certain in his mind,
leading here, surely. It has arrived
at the window, and is clarified.
Now he has learned another way
he can come here. Luck
taught him, and desire.
The snow lies under the woods
and February is ending.
Far off, another way, he hears
the flute of spring,
an old-style traveler,
wandering through the trees.

22.

Still sleeping, he heard
the phoebe call, and woke to it,
and winter passed out of his mind.
The bird, in the high branches
above the road-culvert mouth,
sang to what was sleeping,
two notes, clear and
harsh. The stream came,
full-voiced, down the rocks
out of the woods. The wood ducks
have come back to nest
in the old hollow sycamore.
The window has changed, no longer
remembering, but waiting.

23.

He stood on the ground
and saw his wife borne away
in the air, and suddenly
knew her. It is not the sky
he trusts her to, or her flight,
but to herself as he saw her
turn back and smile. And he
turned back to the buried garden
where the spring flood rose.
The window is made strange
by these days he has come to.
She is the comfort of the rooms
she leaves behind her.

24.

His love returns
and walks among the trees,
a new time lying beneath
the leaves at her feet.
There are songs in the ground

audible to her. She enters
the dark globe of sleep,
waking the treefrogs
whose songs star the silence
in constellations. She wakens
the birds of mornings. The sun
makes a low gentle piping.
The bloodroot rises in its folded
leaf, and there is a tensing
in the woods. There is
no window where she is.
All is clear where the light begins
to dress the branch in green.

25.

The bloodroot is white
in the woods, and men renew
their abuse of the world
and each other. Abroad
we burn and maim
in the name of principles
we no longer recognize in acts.
At home our flayed land
flows endlessly
to burial in the sea.
When mortality is not heavy
on us, humanity is—
public meaninglessness
preying on private meaning.
As the weather warms, the driven
swarm into the river,
pursued by whining engines,
missing the world
as they pass over it,
every man
his own mosquito.

26.

In the heron's eye
is one of the dies of change.
Another
is in the sun.
Each thing is carried
beyond itself.
The man of the window
lives at the edge,
knowing the approach
of what must be, joy
and dread.
Now the old sycamore
yields at its crown
a dead branch.
It will sink like evening
into its standing place.
The young trees rise,
and the dew is on them,
and the heat of the day
is on them, and the dark
—end and beginning
without end.

27.

Now that April with sweet rain
has come to Port Royal again
Burley Coulter rows out
on the river to fish.
He sits all day in his boat,
tied to a willow, his hat
among green branches,
his dark line curving
in the wind. He is one
with the sun.
The current's horses graze
in the shade along the banks.
The watcher leaves his window

and goes out.
He sits in the woods, watched
by more than he sees.
What is his is
past. He has come
to a roofless place
and a windowless.
There is a wild light
his mind loses
until the spring renews,
but it holds his mind
and will not let it rest.
The window is a fragment
of the world suspended
in the world, the known
adrift in mystery.
And now the green
rises. The window has an edge
that is celestial,
where the eyes are surpassed.

East Kentucky, 1967

What vision or blindness lives
here among the broken places
in the smell of burning
and the stench of dead streams
where only machines thrive
on the death of all else?
What vision or blindness
can live in the sight of children
who inherit the eyes of broken men,
and in the sight of farms torn open
where the rich lock like toads
to the backs of the helpless?

To a Siberian Woodsman

(after looking at some pictures in a magazine)

1.

You lean at ease in your warm house at night after supper,
listening to your daughter play the accordion. You smile
with the pleasure of a man confident in his hands, resting
after a day of long labor in the forest, the cry of the saw
in your head, and the vision of coming home to rest.
Your daughter's face is clear in the joy of hearing
her own music. Her fingers live on the keys
like people familiar with the land they were born in.

You sit at the dinner table late into the night with your
    son,
tying the bright flies that will lead you along the forest
    streams.
Over you, as your hands work, is the dream of the still pools.
    Over you is the dream
of your silence while the east brightens, birds waking close
    by you in the trees.

2.

I have thought of you stepping out of your doorway at dawn,
    your son in your tracks.
You go in under the overarching green branches of the forest
whose ways, strange to me, are well known to you as the
    sound of your own voice
or the silence that lies around you now that you have ceased
    to speak,
and soon the voice of the stream rises ahead of you, and you
    take the path beside it.
I have thought of the sun breaking pale through the mists
    over you
as you come to the pool where you will fish, and of the mist
    drifting
over the water, and of the cast fly resting light on the face
    of the pool.

61

3.

And I am here in Kentucky in the place I have made myself
in the world. I sit on my porch above the river that flows
      muddy
and slow along the feet of the trees. I hear the voices of the
      wren
and the yellow-throated warbler whose songs pass near the
      windows
and over the roof. In my house my daughter learns the
      womanhood
of her mother. My son is at play, pretending to be
the man he believes I am. I am the outbreathing of this
      ground.
My words are its words as the wren's song is its song.

4.

Who has invented our enmity? Who has prescribed us
hatred of each other? Who has armed us against each other
with the death of the world? Who has appointed me such
      anger
that I should desire the burning of your house or the
      destruction of your children?
Who has appointed such anger to you? Who has set loose
      the thought
that we should oppose each other with the ruin of forests
      and rivers, and the silence of birds?
Who has said to us that the voices of my land shall be strange
to you, and the voices of your land strange to me?

Who has imagined that I would destroy myself in order to
　　　destroy you,
or that I could improve myself by destroying you? Who has
　　　imagined
that your death could be negligible to me now that I have
　　　seen these pictures of your face?
Who has imagined that I would not speak familiarly with
　　　you,
or laugh with you, or visit in your house and go to work with
　　　you in the forest?
And now one of the ideas of my place will be that you would
　　　gladly talk and visit and work with me.

　　　5.
I sit in the shade of the trees of the land I was born in.
As they are native I am native, and I hold to this place as
　　　carefully as they hold to it.
I do not see the national flag flying from the staff of the
　　　sycamore,
or any decree of the government written on the leaves of the
　　　walnut,
nor has the elm bowed before monuments or sworn the oath
　　　of allegiance.
They have not declared to whom they stand in welcome.

　　　6.
In the thought of you I imagine myself free of the weapons
　　　and the official hates that I have borne on my back
　　　like a hump,
and in the thought of myself I imagine you free of weapons
　　　and official hates,
so that if we should meet we would not go by each other
　　　looking at the ground like slaves sullen under their
　　　burdens,
but would stand clear in the gaze of each other.

7.

There is no government so worthy as your son who fishes with you in silence beside the forest pool.

There is no national glory so comely as your daughter whose hands have learned a music and go their own way on the keys.

There is no national glory so comely as my daughter who dances and sings and is the brightness of my house.

There is no government so worthy as my son who laughs, as he comes up the path from the river in the evening, for joy.

✒ A Discipline

Turn toward the holocaust, it approaches
on every side, there is no other place
to turn. Dawning in your veins
is the light of the blast
that will print your shadow on stone
in a last antic of despair
to survive you in the dark.
Man has put his history to sleep
in the engine of doom. It flies
over his dreams in the night,
a blazing cocoon. O gaze into the fire
and be consumed with man's despair,
and be still, and wait. And then see
the world go on with the patient work
of seasons, embroidering birdsong
upon itself as for a wedding, and feel
your heart set out in the morning
like a young traveler, arguing the world
from the kiss of a pretty girl.
It is the time's discipline to think
of the death of all living, and yet live.

A Poem of Thanks

I have been spared another day
to come into this night
as though there is a mercy in things
mindful of me. Love, cast all
thought aside. I cast aside
all thought. Our bodies enter
their brief precedence,
surrounded by their sleep.
Through you I rise, and you
through me, into the joy
we make, but may not keep.

🎕 Envoy

Love, all day there has been at the edge of my mind
the wish that my life would hurry on,
my days pass quickly and be done,
for I felt myself a man carrying a loose tottering bundle
along a narrow scaffold: if I could carry it
fast enough, I could hold it together to the end.

Now, leaving my perplexity and haste,
I come within the boundaries of your life, an interior
clear and calm. You could not admit me burdened.
I approach you clean as a child of all that has been with me.
You speak to me in the dark tongue of my joy
that you do not know. In you I know
the deep leisure of the filling moon. May I live long.

Books by Wendell Berry

available in paperback editions
from Harcourt Brace Jovanovich, Inc.